ANSEL ADAMS
Photographs of the Southwest

1. *Eagle Dance, San Ildefonso Pueblo, New Mexico, 1928*

2. *Sunrise from South Rim, Grand Canyon National Park, Arizona, 1942*

ANSEL ADAMS
Photographs of the Southwest

Selected photographs made from 1928 to 1968 in

Arizona, California, Colorado, New Mexico, Texas and Utah

with a statement by the photographer

AND

AN ESSAY ON THE LAND
by Lawrence Clark Powell

LITTLE, BROWN AND COMPANY · BULFINCH PRESS · BOSTON · TORONTO · LONDON

3. Wood carving, George Lopez, Cordova, New Mexico, c. 1960

International Standard Book Number 0-8212-0699-0 (hardcover)
International Standard Book Number 0-8212-1574-4 (paperback)
Library of Congress Catalog Card Number 76-10034

Grateful acknowledgment is made to the following for permission to reprint copyrighted material:

Quote on pages 14–15 from *Mission San Xavier del Bac* by Nancy Newhall. Copyright ©1954 by 5 Associates. Reprinted by permission of 5 Associates and the estate of Nancy Newhall.

Quote on page 17 from *Piñon Country* by Haniel Long. Copyright ©1941 by Haniel Long. Reprinted by permission of The Sunstone Press and Anton V. Long.

Quotes on pages 20–21 and page 36 from *Singing For Power* by Ruth Murray Underhill. Copyright ©1966 by Ruth Murray Underhill. Reprinted by permission of the University of California Press.

Quote on page 22 from *Great River* by Paul Horgan. Copyright ©1954 by Paul Horgan. Reprinted by permission of Holt, Rinehart and Winston.

Quote on page 25 from *Taos Pueblo* by Mary Austin and Ansel Adams; quotes on pages 12 and 29–30 from *The Land of Journeys' Ending* by Mary Austin.

Plates 94 and 96 reproduced courtesy of Parasol Press, New York.

Hardcover endpapers: *From Point Imperial, Grand Canyon National Park, Arizona*, 1942

Bulfinch Press is an imprint and trademark of Little, Brown and Company (Inc.)   Published simultaneously in Canada by Little, Brown & Company (Canada) Limited

Printed in the United States of America   Fourth printing, 1990

To Paul Strand

4. *Thunderstorm, Chama Valley, New Mexico, 1937*

My earliest serious photographs of the Southwest were made around 1928 and my most recent in 1975. When working on a definitive project over a span of time, I found the result might be something fresh and unexpected, something filtered through my heart as well as my mind and eye. My Southwest experience has been more or less continuous; the images are arranged for flow of meaning rather than of location and time. What and who make small difference in the presence of the eternal world and the indelible memory of emotional and aesthetic experience.

The selection of the images is a partial perspective of one man's vision and his response to the land and its culture. Difficult decisions were involved in the selections; a thousand photographs clamored for inclusion in the limited pages of the book. The photographer must be resigned to the doctrine that "less is more" (easier said than done!).

Another problem was encountered—how many images previously reproduced should be included? The consensus was that I could not avoid re-using certain photographs, because of their significance to the general theme and their validity as vital elements of the total interpretation. The larger part of the contents has been seldom, if ever, seen or reproduced and it is hoped that the familiar images will appear fresh in their new context.

The perceptive and beautiful Essay on the Land *by Lawrence Clark Powell is an important adjunct to the photographs. The relationship is synergistic; the text does not describe the pictures and the pictures do not illustrate the text. The essay is an experience, a statement born of Powell's comprehension and love of the Southwest. The small illustrations appearing in the text are both informative and decorative, and are not considered as part of the main sequence of larger reproductions in the book.*

I first came to Santa Fe in 1927 with Bertha Pope Damon and friend, and Albert Bender of San Francisco. I had driven Albert many thousands of miles in California; he had a host of friends among artists, writers, and musicians. He was a generous friend of the finest printers of the time and a dedicated bibliophile. No one will ever know the full measure of his contributions—not so much in money (he was not an affluent person) but in imaginative concepts and assignments, introduction of young artists to the right people to nourish their talent and aspirations, encouragement and support of libraries and museums in particular areas of excellence. This was our first trip east of the Sierra and the Cajon Pass. We wanted to see Mary Austin, Witter Bynner, Haniel Long, Andrew Dasburg, and many others who embraced the Southwest spirit in Santa Fe and Taos.

With Albert Bender I met Mary Austin; a life-long collabora-

tion evolved, as well as a close friendship with Bynner. Indeed, the pull of Santa Fe was very strong. When my wife and I decided to leave San Francisco we were torn between the Southwest and Carmel Highlands. The ocean won: I was born and lived almost my entire life by the sea. Yet whenever I return to Santa Fe and other areas of the Southwest, it is, indeed, a homecoming.

I worked with Mary Austin and Frank Applegate on a proposed book on Southwest arts and crafts (unfortunately Mrs. Austin's death terminated the project). During the years 1928 through 1932 at Taos I met Mabel Dodge and Tony Lujan (Mabel, as Tony's wife, persisted in spelling her name Luhan!), John Marin, Georgia O'Keeffe, and Paul Strand. Paul showed me his negatives (he had no prints with him). It was a profound experience and a turning point in my career. For the first time I saw images revealing a powerful perception and conviction. I was turned from a quasi-pictorial approach to a far more precise and austere vision. In 1933, in New York, I met Alfred Stieglitz, the great American photographer (and encourager of Paul Strand and many artists of all mediums). My dedication to straightforward photography was affirmed.

In the late 1930s Beaumont and Nancy Newhall entered my life. Nancy and I collaborated on several books and exhibits, many related to the Southwest. She was a luminous spirit with an excellent mind and scholarly ability. Her text on Mission San Xavier del Bac is a monument to research and compassion. She prepared an article on the Canyon de Chelly for Arizona Highways; she had never visited the place, acquiring her knowledge from books and publications and the photographs I had made of the area. She was widely complimented on the perception and precision of her essay. An author may write in absentia but the photographer must have his camera in the heart of his subject. Nancy's fatal accident on the Snake River in the Tetons—a tree fell without warning on the inflated raft she was riding—was a mindless act of that nature she loved and interpreted with such passion and affection.

I wish to express deepest appreciation to many friends and colleagues for their advice and aid in the production of this book. First among them, those who have gone to the Great Sky: Mary Austin, Witter Bynner, Frank Applegate, and the others who gave me much encouragement in the earlier years. Then my wife Virginia, who patiently supported my wanderings and interest in the Southwest. She is devoted to Southwest Indian and Hispano-American arts and crafts, as well as to the land and its spirit.

President John P. Schaefer of the University of Arizona at Tucson, who initiated the concept of the new Center for Creative Photography at the University, has been a constant source of en-

VIII

couragement and enthusiasm. Paul Forster of San Francisco, who created the handsome and sympathetic design of this book, and George Waters, also of San Francisco, who produced the plates and printed the book with his usual dedication to excellence, deserve high praise.

I wish warmly to thank my assistants here in Carmel—Alan Ross, Norman Locks, Jim Taylor and Phyllis Donohue, who join in making all things possible. Back of all the organization, the checks and balances of complex goals and procedure, are my most potent and creative associates, Bill and Andrea Turnage. Publishing is an increasingly difficult undertaking in these times; the sympathetic understanding of the requirements of quality by my publisher, New York Graphic Society, is deeply appreciated.

As Lawrence Powell implies, wherever one goes in the Southwest one encounters magic, strength, and beauty. Myriad miracles in time and place occur; there is no end to the grandeurs and intimacies, no end to the revival of the spirit which they offer to all. My Southwest experience is tied intimately with many dear friends; their qualities and support are reflected in part throughout this work, illuminating confidence in personal visualizations of the images of nature and of man in this shining and timeless land.

ANSEL ADAMS   Carmel, May 1976

5. *Witter Bynner, Santa Fe, New Mexico, c. 1960*

6. *Ghost Ranch Hills, Chama Valley, New Mexico, 1937*

The Southwest: An Essay on the Land

BY LAWRENCE CLARK POWELL

START with the land. It was here first and it will be here last. I have called it a great dry and wrinkled land. Those are the basic characteristics of the Southwest. Climate and configuration. Absence of abundant rainfall. Vastness of mountains, deserts, and distance under clear skies. Add color, and an abiding Indo-Hispano influence.

Although it is hard to delimit the Southwest—how far northeast does it go?—it is easy to recognize. *Sun, silence, and adobe* is how Charles F. Lummis characterized it. He was its first booster, a tough little Yankee who came in the 1880s walking all the way and writing letters ahead to the *Los Angeles Times*. It was he who gave the Southwest its generic name.

There are two kinds of Southwesterners: native and adopted. The former were here first—Pimas and Papagos, Yumas, Apaches and Navajos, to name the chief tribes. They or their forebears were here as long as 15,000 years ago, and their descendants will probably be here after

Anglos have run out of energy and the means to live in cool and mobile comfort.

Adopted Southwesterners like Lummis can't contain the joy with which the Southwest fills them. Their enthusiasm attracts immigrants. In our time the Southwest is suffering rapid change. Coal-burning power plants multiply and the Four Corners grow dingy. The Grand Canyon is overrun by motorized rafters and transisterites. Our lust for energy dams the rivers. Missile sites, bombing ranges, nuclear testing, and mock desert warfare, all disturb Lummis's classic Southwest. When blowing dust annoys the urbanites, their reaction is to blacktop the desert.

It is a fragile land of an interconnected ecology. The paucity of rainfall creates a delicate balance now threatened by man's thoughtlessness. Yet no culture lasts forever. Like its predecessors—Anasazi, Salado, Hohokam, Mimbres—our urbo-agri-industrial culture too will pass. To understand history is to concede that all cultures end. The poet writes, "The wave falls and the hand falls; thou shalt not always walk in the sun." Our time will probably last longer than any thus far because we are a clever technical people. If we can learn to exploit the sun's energy, we might live by its heat and light for many millennia—but even then not forever, for the sun's life also is limited.

There is a new desire to control the growth we call Progress. The apple ripens, man eats it. The law of growth and hunger. Because the Southwest is enormously beautiful and its climate mostly moderate, people will continue to come to it.

Yet the many changes it undergoes at men's hands will be on the surface. Although the land will be bulldozed, dug up, and pushed around, only a fraction of it will be disturbed. The Southwest is vast. Go on foot as Lummis did in 1884 or as Van Dyke did in 1900, and you will see its varied extent. To run the river on a raft is not to see much. Flying over the Southwest can be a good geography lesson. From the air can be seen why man went where he did, through passes and along river valleys. Man goes where water flows.

On my wall are colored references to this configured Southwest. They are three-dimensional maps of the com-

ponent states that show how the land has determined history.

"In Nueva Granada the land is still supreme," Paul Horgan wrote of the Southwest, and went on to a lyrical description of the colored earth of New Mexico and Arizona, the region I like to call the Heart of the Southwest. "By land," explained Mary Austin, "I mean all those things common to a given region; the flow of prevailing winds, the succession of vegetal cover, the legend of ancient life; and the scene, above everything the magnificently shaped and colored scene." *Sky Determines* is the title and thesis of Ross Calvin's classic book about the Southwest's heavenly weather.

Where is the heart of hearts, the *cor cordium?* I keep moving it around. There are several places throughout the Southwest where it seems that all the power and glory of the world streams through me from the earth back to the sun and where I feel like a channel in which truth and beauty flow.

Mystical? Yes. The Indians have long harmonized with the mysteries of the land. Their mountains were the homes of the gods. As the Greeks deified Olympus, so do the Navajos revere their sacred peaks. The Papagos of south-

7. *Mary Austin, Santa Fe, New Mexico,* c. *1929*

western Arizona look up to the peak of Baboquívari where the gods rule the elements.

Why do I write again about the Southwest? Because I love the land and write from love undertoned by lament. Its immigrants are often spoilers, dependent upon machines for their needs and comforts. Their cities grow like cancers. Their urban towers, incongruous *casas grandes*, could have been erected anywhere in the world. Their cities' streets are impacted with traffic, the skies obscured, the days and nights grown noisy. *Sun, silence, and adobe* are unknown to inhabitants of the concrete.

I am content to live out my life on the *bajada* of the Santa Catalinas, facing south to the mountains of Mexico. Do I proclaim Tucson to be the heart of hearts? It is obviously not the geographical heart, nor is it the spiritual center, which some say is at Oraibi, Shiprock, or Taos Pueblo. Tucson is to me the intellectual heart and I dwell on its slope because the Southwest's major university and research library are nearby. As a writer, my roots are nourished by the records of the past as well as by the beauty of the present.

Thus I live on the edge of the Old Pueblo, a community founded the year before the signing of the Declaration of

Independence. The only competitor for my residential affection is that even older pueblo of Santa Fe. If the City of the Holy Faith had intellectual facilities to equal Tucson's, I could happily live there in the lee of the Sangre de Cristos.

This river-bounded domain of southern Arizona and northern Sonora is the old Pimería Alta—the Land of the Upper Pimas—first civilized by Padre Eusebio Kino, a German-educated Italian who came from Spain in 1687 as a Jesuit missionary, bringing livestock, fruits, and grains to trade for Indian souls. Kino was the first creative Southwesterner and he remains one of the greatest. Although he did not build the Mission San Xavier del Bac in the form we know today, he did found the mission to honor St. Francis Xavier, there on the western bank of the Rio Santa Cruz, at the site of the Papago village of Bac.

Many descriptions of San Xavier have been written by travelers during the past two centuries. None is more glowing than that by the late Nancy Newhall, in a monograph with eloquent photography by Ansel Adams. High Mass moved her to this passage:

"Here the Mission is crowded with a barbarian dusk and shot with startling splendor. Dark massive faces of Papago women under silk kerchiefs of turquoise, emerald, purple. A Mexican beauty in tangerine, with a gold scarf over her head. A little Papago girl with a crown of scarlet poppies on her jet pigtails. Old Papago men in blue jeans, with wide straw hats in their huge hands and silver buckles under their paunches. Yaqui patriarchs, of immense dignity, with long braids tied around their heads with ribbon. A Mexican baby, with a skin like dark cream, in a cloud of a pink dress caught here and there with forget-me-nots. And old women, Mexican and Indian, with their heads draped in black lace mantillas, the lace often hanging down over rough old sweaters or housedresses pale with washing.

"Black-headed babies squall or crow, resisting every effort to hush them. A dog or two wanders in through the open doors, sometimes joining with wagging tail a solemn procession down the aisle. Little Papago acolytes shake their scarlet skirts at him and urge him off with a surreptitious foot, usually in vain. It does not matter; nothing mars the great prayer of the Mass.

"Overhead, serene and luminous, rise the arches and the domes. And now the celestial court—the angels, the flying cherubim, the saints appearing in their niches, the Mother and Son—seem strange no longer. They have become one indivisible universe with their worshippers, their rich setting no more bizarre than this their congregation.

"Out in the sun again, the dark faces and the gemlike colors are seen to be native to the desert plain, the sharp peaks, the immense horizons."

Last Christmas Eve I attended midnight Mass at San Xavier. The floodlit mission, visible from afar, was truly the White Dove of the Desert. By eleven o'clock the nave and transept were crowded, and I stood against the wall by the crèche. Since this is the mission church of San Xavier Reservation, most of the celebrants were Papagos. The red-robed acolytes' round brown faces shone with mingled awe and mischief as they tended the priest while he placed the babe in the hammock of the crèche.

All were transfixed. Smoke from the priest's censer rose to the arches and the painted vault of the roof. The choir sang in unison. The bread was broken, the wine drunk. As lips touched and hands clasped, a wave of love surged through the church. It was Epiphany, as Christ spoke with the inner voice.

The church emptied into the night. Frost had begun to form. The bittersweet smell of burning mesquite filled the

8. *Angel, Mission San Xavier del Bac, Tucson, Arizona, c. 1950*

air. A half moon rose over the hill. The celebrants went their ways into desert and town.

ii

How should one first come to the Southwest? There are various ways, all beautiful, some more dramatic. The southern routes are the subtlest. There the plains of Texas and Oklahoma merge with those of New Mexico. Between the pages of one of my books is pressed a florarium of Highway 54, fragile evidence that all the flowers of summer once lit this way southwest.

If one comes by Roswell on the Pecos, one finds Paul Horgan–Peter Hurd country. Their stories and paintings were created here. The road tracks northwest across grasslands and up Hondo Creek into the Sacramentos, past San Patricio where Peter Hurd now lives. Then it crosses the Mescalero Apache reservation and drops into the Tularosa basin, a *bolsón* or pocket between the Sacramento and the San Andrés ranges.

Hurd and Horgan celebrated those lands east of the mountains; Tularosa is the domain of Eugene Manlove Rhodes, the only rangeland peer of Arizona's Ross Santee —both men with power over cattle, horses, and words.

Rhodes lies buried high in the San Andrés mountains. The road to his grave crosses the White Sands, now a missile range closed to public access.

Trinity Site is nearby, where The Bomb was first exploded. Man's compulsion to create and destroy distinguishes this place. Over it rises Sierra Blanca, high landmark of southeastern New Mexico. On its shoulder is the village of Cloudcroft, as poetically named as Arizona's Snowflake (the charm of which is somewhat lessened when we know that it was named for two worthy Mormons, Mr. Snow and Mr. Flake).

Rhodes's pocket empties into Texas's outpost of El Paso. Three Texans glorify that city—Hertzog the printer, Lea the writer-painter, and Cisneros the illustrator. No other southwestern city can boast such a creative trio. Their collaboration somewhat gentles this rough Texan counterpart of Albuquerque and Phoenix.

The mountains of southern Arizona hardly rival the Rockies. The sandy wastes of the southwestern corner are beautiful only to a viewer with time and lenses to look at them long and lovingly as Joseph Wood Krutch did. In the final twenty years of his life, that transplanted philosopher-naturalist was the conscience-voice of the Southwest.

South from Willcox the road runs to the Mexican border. To the west lies a *playa* that rainfall turns into a shallow lake. To the east are the Chiricahuas, the former domain of Cochise and his Apache raiders. It is a lonely road. Few travel this route to the twin border cities of Douglas and Agua Prieta. All the land of southern Arizona rises gradually from the Gila River valley. Sage and juniper yield to grama grass and oak. Cattle fatten on a range enriched by the rainy seasons of summer and winter.

The high stack of the smelter heralds the company town of Douglas, where coffee may be taken at the opulent Gadsden Hotel. Beyond in Bisbee, the Lavender Pit could have served Doré as a coppery model for his hellish drawings. The old Copper Queen Hotel offers hospitality, although Bisbee suffers from a dwindling supply of profitable ore.

The road leads back to Tucson through Tombstone on its high mesquite mesa and over the grasslands and oak groves which lie between the Whetstones and the Santa Ritas. This is an Arizona without the dramatic appeal of the Painted Desert or the Grand Canyon; it is a grassy land of peace and plenty.

The northern ways are more thrilling. They come through the passes of Raton and Wolf Creek. The former is the old Santa Fe Trail that led from the Missouri frontier by Las Vegas to the City of the Holy Faith. At trail's end is piñon and juniper country where the earth is reddish, the vegetation dark green. It was near here at Laguna that Haniel Long, the sage of Santa Fe, first came under the spell of the Southwest.

"I stepped down into the freshness and vastness of the diminutive piñon forest," he recalled, "and as I walked about among the blue-green odorous trees, I felt like a giant, for over their heads was the horizon of the mountains. On a nearby hill was the ancient town, the first pueblo I had ever seen. I was pleased that houses could be so unpretentious, built simply of the earth and leaving nothing to be improved upon. So with the little trees: they gave me the pleasure that comes of small perfect things which adapt their forces without scattering or waste."

Coming east from California, the dramatic route is over the Sierra Nevada via Tioga Pass and the abrupt drop into the Owens River valley. Ansel Adams photographed these mountains and this valley for an edition of Mary Austin's *The Land of Little Rain*. It is a land akin to northern New Mexico, and the Sierra Nevada is a big brother to the Sangre de Cristo. The valley's villain is Los Angeles, which bought up the land and aqueducted its water. In her outrage, Mary Austin foretold doom for the Angel City. She probably meant earthquake and fire. Having covered the destruction of San Francisco in 1906 for Lummis's *Out West*, she knew what can happen to a city when the earth shakes and burns. Now Los Angeles's end may come from overpopulation, industrialization, and pollution. Choking and smothering also spell doom.

From the Owens River valley the road crosses the Panamints and Death Valley, through lands of less than little rain. The first collaboration between Ansel Adams and Nancy Newhall produced a beautiful book on Death Valley. The sculptor Gordon Newell lives in the Panamints with stone for his chisel and unlimited crystal air of a clean world. "When you tell about this beautiful part of the Southwest," he wrote me, "consider the thought that 'Death Valley' is a misnomer, for that is where Life best demonstrates its ability to survive. From pupfish to creosote, a continuity persists that belies the name 'Death.' That a few confused tourists left their bones there is pretty irrelevant in the scale and scheme of time and weather."

Where Utah yields the Strip to Arizona, the land rises onto the forested Kaibab plateau to end at the North Rim of the Grand Canyon. From there the Bright Angel trail drops, crosses the river, and climbs to the South Rim. Although it is only a dozen miles across, by car it takes hours to drive the two hundred miles around this deep wound in the earth's body.

I was on the South Rim at Christmastime. Snow shrouded the canyon as I walked along the edge at twilight in a thin fall of flakes. Sweet chimney smoke filled the air, and that smell of burning pinewood recalled my childhood transits of territory when the incense of sawmill meant that California came on the morrow.

A darkened building proved to be the studio of the Kolb brothers, the early river-runners and photographers. There on display was the very boat that had carried them through the Grand Canyon from Wyoming to Mexico. Ellsworth Kolb's book of their adventure was my first Southwest book. It was a gift from my father on my fifteenth birthday, a few months before his early death. I have kept it as a talisman.

There are other gifts that I cherish from my father's travels in the Southwest. One is an Apache basket that he bought at the Fred Harvey shop in The Alvarado at Albuquerque. Before that beautiful hotel was bulldozed for a parking lot, I often went there just to watch the passing trains. Albuquerqueans were wont to set their watches by those Santa Fe trains: *California Limited*, *Scout*, *Missionary*, *Navajo*, *Chief*, *Super Chief*, and *El Capitan*. Once when speaking to a conference at The Alvarado, I paused upon hearing the sigh of relaxing Westinghouses. "What train is that?" I asked the chairman. He pulled out his watch. "Eastbound mail," he said. I resumed my talk.

iii

I have taken my place in the company of travelers in the Southwest, and I go with their books in my baggage and their ghosts at my side. They are friendly ghosts. Some are heroic, more are obscure. First came Don Francisco Vasquez de Coronado. Although he did not find the Golden Cities of Cíbola (they proved to be the adobe pueblos of the Indians), Coronado surely had a great trip. If there was no poetry in him when in 1540 he and his men marched up the valley of the San Pedro, deep into Arizona and New Mexico and as far as the present-day Nebraska, was he indifferent to the sky's blueness and its glitter at night? To his dying day did he not remember the smell of mesquite with which his men made their fires? Four hundred and thirty-six years later, the valley of the San Pedro is still thicketed with huge mesquites. If Coronado came for gold and Kino for God, now in our time the poet and the photographer come for the glory of form and color of earth and sky.

Earlier in that same century the mystical healer Alvar Nuñez Cabeza de Vaca also came this way, one of the last survivors of a shipwreck on the Florida coast. It took those wanderers eight years to cross the continent, during which they discovered they had the power to heal the sick. If I were to choose a single masterpiece of Southwest literature it might be Haniel Long's *Interlinear to Cabeza de Vaca*, a prose poem that extracts the inner meaning of the Spaniards' odyssey. "Crack the rock if so you list," wrote another poet, "bring to light the amethyst." This Long did in his jewel of a book.

In later centuries there came the Jesuit Kino, and Anza, the Sonoran commander, and Garcés, the Franciscan priest. It was Garcés who crept to the bottom of the Grand Canyon and in 1776 rode his mule into Oraibi on that fateful fourth day of July. He was turned away by the Hopis. They preferred their gods to his.

My roll call of heroes includes Kearny, who seized the

Southwest from Mexico; Cooke, who blazed the first wagon road to the Pacific; and the Apache chiefs Mangas Coloradas and Cochise, fighters to hold their domain. "I think continually of those who were truly great," wrote Stephen Spender; and as I travel in the Southwest, I re-people it with its heroic leaders. With them at my side, I am never alone nor lonely.

West-southwest of Tucson, the Papaguería yields to Sonora. This is still the domain of Padre Kino, although three centuries have passed since he came this way on foot and horseback, setting records of endurance that have never been equaled. The Papagos are a solid race whose bulk conceals their poetic legendry. "People of the Crimson Evening," they have been called. Their land was not coveted by conquistadors, missionaries, gold seekers, or settlers.

"So the Papagos wandered, calm and smiling, back and forth across the waste of brilliant barrenness," wrote anthropologist Ruth Underhill. "They shot the ground squirrels and the rats and birds. They picked the caterpillars from the bushes. They shook the seeds from every blade of wild grass. They brushed the spines from cactus stems and roasted them for hours in a pit with a fire over it. I have never heard one of them object to this plan of life.

9. *Baboquívari Peak, Arizona, 1965*

Rather, an old woman telling me of it sighed and said: 'To you Whites, Elder Brother gave wheat and peaches and grapes. To us, he gave the wild seeds and the cactus. Those are the *good* foods.' "

The peak of Baboquívari rises above the desert floor to visibility for a hundred miles around. At the other end of the range stands Kitt Peak, upon which astronomers have built a great national observatory. "Men with Long Eyes," the Papagos call them. In granting the scientists rights on their mountain, the Indians retained those to the native wood—the slow-burning, gray-barked Arizona oak, *Quercus Arizonica Sargent.*

There are many devices on Kitt Peak whereby astronomers scan the sky. I leave them to their devices. When I go up the mountain, it is to picnic among the jay-haunted oaks. In the summertime the air is cool up there. The ground is strewn with tiny acorns. I once saw children gathering them, and this dialogue took place:

"What are you going to do with those acorns?" I asked.

"Sell them to neighborhood children."

"For how much?"

"A penny a handful."

"May I buy some?"

The children thought a minute and then one said, "No."

"Why not?"

"Your hands are too big."

iv

Arizona and New Mexico display great cultural differences. The former is Indo-Anglo, the latter Indo-Hispano. The reason is a river and its valley, the Rio Grande, New Mexico's great river along which Indians, Spaniards, and Mexicans have acculturated for a thousand years. Arizona has no such valleys with gentle gradient and sides. Until dammed, its great rivers, the Colorado and the Gila, were wild rivers. No culture could root in their savage depths and flooded widths.

The continuity of life along the Rio Grande and its tributaries gave New Mexico a richness not present in any other part of the Southwest. That culture endures to this day. There are eighteen hundred miles of river from Boca del Rio, where the Rio Grande debouches into the Gulf of Mexico, to its source in the Colorado Rockies.

I know the Rio Grande only from the point in Texas where the Pecos flows into the greater river; and I know it best between Albuquerque and where the river engorged itself into the volcanic plain. From there I take off on roads high into the ranges on either side.

History has touched this valley long and lightly. Like the Papaguería, it was never raped. No desirable metals were unearthed there. Water is the only precious element. The Rio Grande is a perennial stream, fed by the eternal snows and springs of the San Juan Rockies. In spring the river's course is green, in autumn gold, in winter bare. Cottonwoods are the predominant trees. In his history of the Rio Grande, Paul Horgan writes lyrically of the cottonwood:

"Its wood was soft and manageable, and it supplied material for many objects. Its silver bark, its big, varnished leaves sparkling in the light of summer and making caverns of shade along the banks, its winter-hold of leaves the color of beaten thin gold lasting in gorgeous bounty until the new catkins of spring—all added grace to the pueblo world. The columnar trunks were used to make tall drums, hollowed out and resonated with skins stretched over the open ends. The wood was hot fuel, fast-burning, leaving a pale, rich ash of many uses. Even the catkins had personal use—eaten raw, they were a bitter delicacy in some towns.

And in that arid land, any tree, much less a scattered few, or a bounteous grove, meant good things—water somewhere near, and shade and shelter from the beating sun and talk from trifling leaves."

The Indian pueblos line the river from Isleta to Taos. The latter had to leave the gorge to find its water along a tributary. At Cochití Pueblo the Jemez range forms the western wall. A rocky road climbs to the plateau from juniper through piñon and ponderosa to aspen and spruce. It is a steep road, patrolled by squirrels and bluejays. History has overlooked this lonely canyon.

The road leads to a place where history came with terrible impact: the Los Alamos laboratories of the Atomic Energy Commission. Here The Bomb was built. The shock waves from its detonation are still traveling.

The road down from the Pajarito plateau crosses the river at Otowi. There during the war, Edith Warner and an Indian from the nearby pueblo of San Ildefonso had a tearoom to which the scientists came for relaxation. She knew that it was a holy place. The presence of water in an arid land—a river, a spring, a fountain, or an oasis—means that the gods are near. "This morning I stood on the river bank to pray," Peggy Pond Church quotes Edith Warner in *The House at Otowi Bridge*, tenderest of Southwest classics. "I knew then that the ancient ones were wise to pray for peace and beauty and not for specific gifts, except fertility which is continued life."

What a strange conjunction is that of Los Alamos and San Ildefonso, of laboratory and pueblo! The latter is an idyllic place of dusty plaza, kiva, and cottonwood. It is the home of Maria the potter, who lives on into her nineties. Nearby are the candlemakers called the Wicked Wicks. With that many candles to burn, who would begrudge a burner at both ends?

The road back to Santa Fe passes the outdoor opera theater. There I was so bemused one summer by the soaring ecstasy of *Der Rosenkavalier* that I had almost to be helped to my car by a sweet usher from Española. There during the entr'acte may be seen a fashion show of capes and cloaks, of silks and corduroys, in all the colors worn by cloth. Chromatics to match the music.

In Santa Fe, bronze plaques commemorate Stravinsky's presence in the 1960s when his Mass was sung in the cathedral—Archbishop Lamy's cathedral of St. Francis. When the first traders came in the 1820s, they found no trees to

10. *Maria Martinez, potter, San Ildefonso Pueblo, New Mexico, c. 1929*

11. *Frank Applegate, Santa Fe, New Mexico, c. 1930*

shade the dusty lanes and bare plaza. In *Commerce of the Prairies*, Gregg described Santa Fe as a huddle of mud houses, hardly the New Jerusalem.

Today, the city is a green park, guarded by the Sangre de Cristo range, the final thrust of the Rockies. Quaking aspens band the conifered mountainside, a stand that established itself where a fire once burned the evergreens. The leaves of *Populus tremuloides* are never still. They tremble even when there seems to be no movement of the air.

The road to Taos follows the river past orchards of apple and cherry, at last to gain the plain. The wise traveler pauses there to see a view like none other in the Southwest. It was D. H. Lawrence's favorite vista, across the gray-green sage—*Artemesia tridentata*—and golden-flowered rabbit brush to the blueness of Lobo Peak, Taos Mountain, and the gorge of the Rio Grande.

Taos was once the rendezvous of the trappers known as Mountain Men. In our time, poets, painters, photographers, and writers have been drawn there. Mabel Dodge and Tony Lujan, Mary Austin, Willa Cather, Frank Applegate, Edward Weston, and Ansel Adams are among those who have come and gone.

It was at Taos and Santa Fe that Ansel Adams first saw

the Southwest. The time was the spring of 1927. By a coincidence, it was the very season and year that I first came to the Southwest—to the Old Pueblo of Tucson. His visit resulted in a Grabhorn Press book now of legendary rarity. It includes Ansel Adams's photographs and Mary Austin's essay on Taos Pueblo. Genius has never been more happily wed. Nowhere else did she write prose of such precise and poetical authority.

"Always for the most casual visitor at Taos, there is the appeal of strangeness; the dark people, the alien dress, the great house-heaps intricately blocked in squares of shadow and sunlight on tawny earthen walls." And then follows a calendar of seasonal vegetation. "Thickets of wild plums abound there, tangles of virgin's bower, meadow sweet, wild iris, blue bush lupins, and tufted grass. It is the wild plums that continue the note of aliveness, the sense of things going on, of contriving, which is so characteristic of the Taos Valley scene." And so on through summer, fall, and winter. Their *Taos Pueblo* is a true and beautiful book by two consummate artists.

Now, half a century later, Taos teems with tourists in summer and skiers in winter. They trail fumes and leave their eternal litter. "Who killed Taos?" "I," said Cock

12. *Tony Lujan, Taos Pueblo, New Mexico*, c. *1930*

Car, "I killed Taos with my internal combustion engine."

There is a long way back to Santa Fe. It heads north to Questa, then ascends the Red River (the little Red) past the molybdenum mine and over the pass in the lee of Mount Wheeler, New Mexico's highest point, to Eagle Nest Lake, Guadalupita, and Mora (all deep Penitente country) and down to Las Vegas and La Galeria de los Artesanos on the plaza in Old Town, a charming shop of books and crafts. The region's master novelist is Frank Waters. The Taos Indian mystique is the theme of *The Man Who Killed the Deer*, while in *People of the Valley*, Waters tenderly delineates the Hispano mores.

Here at Las Vegas, Kearny seized the Southwest for the United States when Governor Armijo prudently gave up without a fight. The Santa Fe Trail is now Interstate 25, and it follows the railroad known as Amtrak. I prefer to call it the Atchison, Topeka and Santa Fe, and I still think of its somewhat less than crack train as the *Super Chief*. Over these rails I first came west at the age of four months to seek my fortune.

Ribera is the double-tracked midpoint between Chicago and Los Angeles where the east-west trains meet. First one hears the growl of approaching Diesels. The eastbound's

13. *Jose Dolores Lopez, wood carver, Cordova, New Mexico, 1928*

is deeper because the grade is rising toward Raton. Then the opposing trains appear. Capped and gloved on their thrones, the engineers salute. Porters lean from open vestibules and trade fond obscenities. Passengers are unaware of the encounter. I alone witness that orgasmic meeting of the silvery trains.

If history has been gentle to the Rio Grande's valley, the tributaries and uplands have not been touched at all. Above Española, life goes on as it has for centuries. Cottonwoods change their leaves with the seasons. Cherries flower and fruit and go bare. Apples ripen and fall. Red peppers hang in strings, then are ground into fiery powder. The houses of stone or adobe have steep roofs for snow to slide off. Piñon smoke sweetens the air. Although not the heart of the wide Southwest, this is surely New Mexico's heartland. If Coronado, Oñate, or Vargas came this way as they did so long ago, they would again call it New Spain, so much does it resemble the land of the mother country.

My destination is the Santuario of Chimayó, a primitive chapel with a healing shrine. Votive offerings and discarded crutches bear witness to pilgrims' faith. Two cottonwoods once guarded the sanctuary. Now only one remains, watered by an *acéquia* that flows past its base. The stump of the other could serve as a picnic table for the weary suppliant.

From Chimayó the road climbs barren hills to the hogback village of Truchas, the Trout. Here in the high foothills of the Sangre de Cristos the roofs have an even steeper pitch. In the east rise the peaks of Truchas, second highest mountain in New Mexico. Beyond is the Pecos wilderness, fairest of Southwest uplands.

I have friends in Truchas, a mother and son who are the third and fourth generation of weavers. Her grandfather taught her to spin and weave in their natal village of Córdova. The mother's fingers are nimbler, the son's legs stronger as he dances on the treadle. In early autumn the shop is sun-warmed, while through the open window smoke drifts from cooking fires. Piñon, of course. Piles of it are stacked throughout the village. The peaks of Truchas rise heavenward. The universe stands still.

Is this journey's end? No, I have one more village to visit. Trampas, the Traps. Beavers were once taken here, hence the name. A small plaza, a little church whose bells have been removed for safekeeping. The one called Grácia (from its sweet tone) I once made ring with a rap of my knuckles. Good works were done here by Anglo architects. Nathanael Owings kept a road-widening from threatening the

14. *Cross, Las Trampas, New Mexico,* c. *1960*

chapel; John Gaw Meem mercifully restored the towers.

On the edge of the village is a little masterpiece of hydraulic engineering—a *canoa*, or canoe, made of hollowed-out cottonwood logs. It carries water to the villagers' fields and orchards. I stop there to drink. A bluebird does the same.

"How old is that *canoa?*" I asked my friend Orlando from Nambé.

"Who knows?" the young Hispano replied. "My grandfather says his grandfather once helped replace the rotting logs. I think it is as old as Time itself."

v

From afar the Southwest appears even more enchantingly configured and colorful. At least it did to me during absence in New England. Winter was snowy, spring rainy, the summer humid. I longed for what, in his exile from New Mexico, Eugene Manlove Rhodes called "the glowing heart of the world."

And so I left Boston with no regret on the drive west-southwest. Each night holed up in a motel, I mapped the morrow's journey deeper into the heartland. In St. Louis I paused to see the fountain of fountains—Carl Milles's "The

Meeting of the Waters," a great bronze group personifying the confluence of the Missouri and the Mississippi. There under a windy sky I spent an hour marveling at the life-sized figures of river god and goddess, tritons and naiads, fishes and shells—and getting soaked by the ever-shifting spray from the fountain's jets. Here was water to waste. Here the plenty of the country's greatest rivers makes water a common element. My thirst was for the arid lands where water is more precious than copper or gold.

From Denver I crossed South Park and ascended the Arkansas, climbed over Independence Pass and dropped down on Aspen, a mountain village that, like Taos, has suffered from pleasure seekers and the franchise wolves who come after them. I went on soon to Alamosa on the upper Rio Grande. Here the river is restrained by a weir to form a backwater for birds and boys with boats. On above, the stream narrows toward its source in the San Juans, flowing fast and tracking glitter in the early sunlight.

I climbed the road up South Fork, rising to the roar of white water and over Wolf Creek Pass and the continental divide where the view is far down on the first meander of the San Juan. To tarry there above tree line in summer is to call down the lightning, and so I switch-backed on to Pagosa Springs and on west to Durango and the Mesa Verde.

There at the matrix of Pueblo culture, I had reached the farthest north of my Southwest. Was it the prolonged drought of the thirteenth century that forced the dwellers to trek south to the Pajarito plateau and the Rio Grande and there re-establish their culture? No one knows for sure. On my first visit to the Mesa Verde many years before, I had a fleeting vision of the people of Spruce Tree House, climbing down the ladders and filing away, carrying little food and no water. I communed then with the mystique of the land. A beautiful expression of it is Mary Austin's *The Land of Journeys' Ending*, its prose lit by poetic insight as in this passage:

"Walking there, one of these wide-open summer days, when there comes a sudden silence, and in the midst of the silence a stir, look where you walk. If your feet stumble in a round depression, to the north of which you discover squarish, low mounds of reddish rock; if, beyond the margin of shallow basins, you observe windrows of loose stones pitched out from between the hills of corn long before the leveled space was taken by three-hundred-year-old pines, know that you are in the country of the Smallhouse People.

Always, incredibly, there lingers about these places, where once was man, some trace that the human sense responds to, never so sensitively as where it has lain mellowing through a thousand years of sun and silence."

The road leads south to Shiprock. Geologists call it a basalt plug. To the Navajos it was their salvation from the warlike Utes. When they sought refuge on it, the rock soared and bore them away to a safer land. No wonder they hold it sacred.

I passed Shiprock on the hundred-mile run to Gallup, that rough railroad town on the edge of the Navajo reservation. Here the Indian may be seen in the stages of disintegration—drinking, fighting, staggering, and falling to sidewalk and gutter. Here is the place to read *Laughing Boy*, La Farge's lament for a people debauched by an alien race. If the Navajos would recover their pride and become The Nation they call themselves, they should build a great wall between them and such towns.

My destination lay farther south at El Morro, the national monument called Inscription Rock, a buff-colored battlement of sandstone upon which passing travelers from the time of Don Juan de Oñate in 1605 have left their presence carved in the stone. *Pasó por aquí*—came this way—they declared. I once romantically proclaimed El Morro to be the Southwest's heart of hearts. Nowhere is there a better refuge from the threats of modern life. Few people go there. There are no lodgings, no concessions, nothing but a small museum and a vast sense of history. El Morro has been protected since President Theodore Roosevelt's time against all enemies save the wind and the rain.

Lummis photographed El Morro and called it The Great Stone Autograph Album. Mary Austin longed to be buried there. "Here at least I shall haunt," she wrote in *The Land of Journeys' Ending*, "and as the time-streams bend and swirl about the Rock, I shall see again all the times that I have loved, and know certainly all that I now guess at. . . . You, of a hundred years from now, if when you visit the Rock, you see the cupped silken wings of the argemone burst and float apart when there is no wind; or if, when all around is still, a sudden stir in the short-leaved pines, or fresh eagle feathers blown upon the shrine, that will be I, making known in such fashion as I may, the land's undying quality."

I have climbed to the top of El Morro and rested there with bluebird and butterfly and the shade of Mary Austin. Beyond to the east sits the old Acoma Pueblo, brooding,

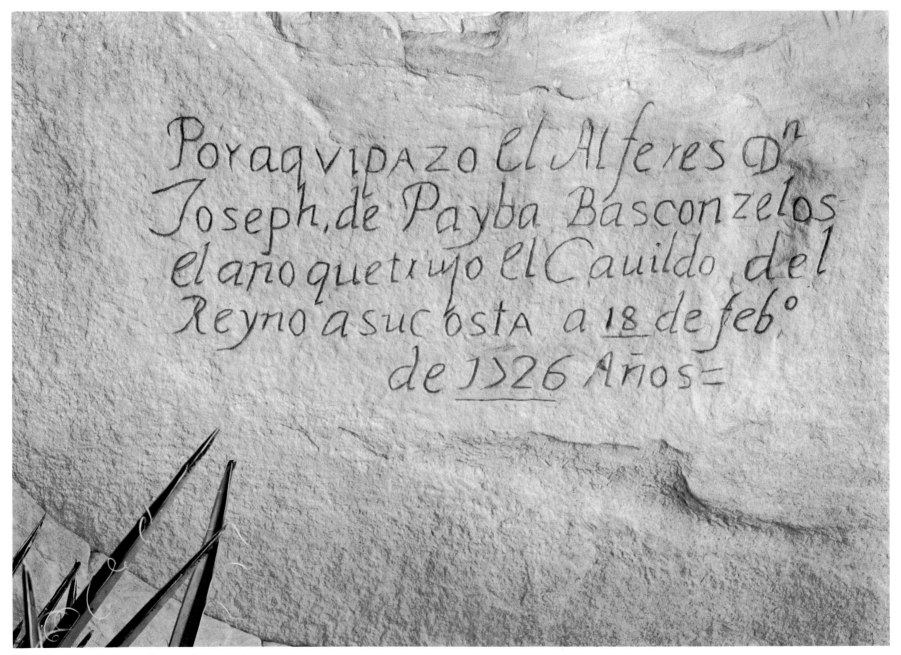

15. *Spanish inscription, El Morro National Monument, New Mexico, c. 1948*

timeless; Zuñi lies to the west. It is land of beautiful choices.

vi

"Water is what these Indians worship," Coronado reported to his viceroy, "because they say it is what makes the corn grow." The early Spaniards observed that the natives' worship included the offering of painted sticks, plumes, powders made of yellow flowers, and pieces of turquoise which were placed by springs.

The Indians still acknowledge the divinity of water. The Hopis employ serpentine rituals to call down the rain. The Papagos sing for power over the essential element.

Anglos also recognize water as the Southwest's basic element. Who owns water, owns all. They have made it serve us with dams and canals to create power and irrigate crops. Yet they waste water as if it were an inexhaustible resource. They fail to realize that there could come another drought such as the one that ended human life on the Mesa Verde.

The water gods must be propitiated. One way is for each community in the arid lands to dedicate a fountain to the divinity of water. Where water is abundant, as in St. Louis, a fountain is less meaningful, beyond the mere beauty of it, than a fountain where water is scarce. Southwesterners should be taught from childhood that the source of their water lies beyond the faucet.

I have gone time and again to the great river dams of the Southwest—to Laguna, Imperial, Hoover, and Glen Canyon on the Colorado; to Roosevelt on the Salt, Coolidge on the Gila, and to Elephant Butte on the Rio Grande. Only for two—Laguna and Roosevelt—do I have especial affection. Is it because they were the only ones known to my father? To them he made the hard journey by mule-drawn wagon that was necessary in 1909.

Laguna and Roosevelt were the first dams to be constructed under the Reclamation Act of 1902. Then a horticulturist in the United States Department of Agriculture, my father came from Washington to inspect these new sources of life and light and power.

Laguna Dam on the Colorado above Yuma was originally a mile-wide, Indian weir-type barrier of rock and brush, meant to restrain the river's spring flooding and to furnish water for crops on reclaimed desert land. Laguna was eventually made obsolete by nearby Imperial Dam.

I have gone there on the river in the blazing heat of August. Now motorized campers abound. Few if any know the history and meaning of man's achievement in subduing the Colorado. None knows why I go there with thankful heart to honor my father and to marvel at the hydraulics. Sluiced water roars into the desilting basins and is canalled into the Imperial Valley of California to irrigate carrots, cotton, melons, and lettuce. Birds bob on the lake. Arrow weed and tules line the banks. The mountains look as if they had been cut out of cardboard. The air shimmers with heat.

East of Phoenix the road leads to the junction where the Apache Trail enters the domain of the Tonto Apaches. Men of that tribe were a main source of labor when Roosevelt Dam was built during the years 1905-1911. President Theodore Roosevelt himself, for whom it was named, dedicated the dam with a moving peroration:

"I do not know if it is of any consequence to a man whether he has a monument. I know it is of mighty little consequence whether he has a statue after he is dead. If there could be any monument which would appeal to any man, surely it is this. You could not have done anything which would have pleased and touched me more than to name this great dam, this great reservoir site, after me, and I thank you from my heart for having done so."

Then and now, Theodore Roosevelt Dam is the greatest masonry dam in the world, built of sandstone blocks quarried from the very walls of the canyon whose river, the Salt, is dammed. This majestic barrier has meant more to Arizona than any other single undertaking. By its mastery of the Salt and the lower Gila, the city of Phoenix and the surrounding Valley of the Sun were made to flourish and be fruitful.

I have gone there to Roosevelt Dam in all seasons. In winter the land is the most beautiful, its strong colors subdued and made restful to the eyes. Then are seen soft greens, browns, and blues under gray skies. The water behind the dam is then olive green instead of the blue of summer.

Coolidge Dam on the Gila lies southeast of Roosevelt Dam. It was built of concrete of an odd bulbous design. From a vantage point downstream, the dam's face is seen to be ornamented with great cement eagles. Green water from the penstocks streams languidly into the canyon that carries it through the mountains to the lower lands it irrigates.

Lake San Carlos is fed by the capricious Gila that rises in the wilderness of the Arizona–New Mexico boundary. When Coolidge Dam was dedicated in 1927, the water was very low, a circumstance that led Will Rogers to quip to President Coolidge, "If this was my lake, I'd mow it."

Few people go there except to fish in the lake. In summer the heat is fierce. Then the sotol sends up its golden-candled stalk. The Pinals dance in the sun. This is the land celebrated by Ross Santee—horse-wrangler, artist, writer, laureate of the Arizona range.

vii

Each of us seeks his state of grace. I have tendered here ways by which I have found mine. The Southwest has many hearts, synchronized by configuration and color. Even though we cannot define and delimit the Southwest to the satisfaction of all its lovers, we all know when we have reached it, whether it be west of the Pecos, south of the Mesa Verde, east of the Sierra Nevada and the Colorado, or north of the Sonoran rivers and the mountains of Chihuahua.

Salmon-colored cliffs, dove-colored deserts, rocky peaks and wooded ranges; hogans, wickiups, ramadas, and concrete towers; dust storms, flash floods, and red skies at morn and evening—nowhere do they come together with such beautiful meaning as they do in the Southwest.

Whose Southwest is it? Does it belong to the Indians?

They were here first. Yet they were not always here. They too came from elsewhere, from South America or Asia. So did cattle, sheep, and horses. Then what *is* native? Ocotillo and saguaro. Copper, gold, and turquoise. The horned toad and the cactus wren and the rivers that run when the weather comes from off the ocean of storms.

The Papagos have always known from where the weather comes. In ancient times when they made their annual journey to the Pacific for salt, they sang this song:

By the sandy water I breathe in the smell of the sea,
From there the wind comes and blows over the world.
By the sandy shore I breathe in the smell of the sea,
From there the clouds come and rain falls over the world.

When one is far from the Southwest or when one is no longer able to roam, how can one best evoke the colored lands? Imagination serves. Photographs help. On walls at home one can see Shiprock at sunrise, the White Sands by moonlight, or the towers of the White Dove and the helmet of Baboquívari.

Maps lend the illusion of distance. There is a geological map of Arizona in pastel colors to delight as well as inform.

And paintings that exalt our view of earth and sky. Maynard Dixon is my favorite painter of the Southwest. His technique was ever equal to his vision. He never stopped growing as an artist, so that the work of his old age was the most daring of all. Navajo painters portray horses as winged creatures of light. Painting is an act of worship and glorification.

There are simpler evocators of the Southwest. Copper lumps and chunks of turquoise. Blue shells from the gulf and bits of petrified wood from the Painted Desert. White sands of gypsum trickling through the hourglass. Or a page from the Northland Press up in Coconino County.

Books are truly the Southwest's most magical surrogates. We have only to read them and be transported onto the continuum of history that carries us back to when man first entered this great old dry and wrinkled land.

16. *Maynard Dixon, painter, Tucson, Arizona, c. 1944*

"*. . . I see*
Many clouds arise.
In front of the sky they lie.
With a good sound
   it is thundering nearby."

PAPAGO SONG

17. *Thunderstorm, Española Valley, New Mexico,* c. *1961*

18. *Spanish Peaks, Colorado,* c. *1951*

19. *Cliff Palace ruin, Mesa Verde National Park, Colorado, 1942*

20. *Tom Reed mine, near Oatman, Arizona, 1952*

21. *Old hearse, Bodie, California,* c. *1940*

22. *Manly Beacon, Death Valley National Monument, California*, c. *1952*

23. *Bad Water, Death Valley National Monument, California,* c. *1952*

24. *Rocks, Joshua Tree National Monument, California*, c. 1942

25. *Rocks, near Tuba City, Arizona,* c. 1950

26. *Cliffs and arroyo, Capitol Reef National Monument, Utah, c. 1947*

27. *Formations, Bryce Canyon National Park, Utah, 1947*

28. *Sand dunes, White Sands National Monument, New Mexico, c. 1942*

29. Goosenecks of the San Juan River, Utah, c. 1940

30. *Canyon de Chelly National Monument, Arizona,* c. 1947

31. *White House ruin, Canyon de Chelly National Monument, Arizona,* c. 1942

32. *Rock formations, Canyon de Chelly National Monument, Arizona,* C. 1947

33. *Rock formations, Canyon de Chelly National Monument, Arizona,* c. 1947

34. *Aspen grove, North Rim, Grand Canyon National Park, Arizona,* c. 1942

35. *Cape Royal, from South Rim, Grand Canyon National Park, Arizona, c. 1947*

36. *Sunrise, Laguna Pueblo, New Mexico*, c. 1942

37. *Pool, Acoma Pueblo, New Mexico,* c. *1942*

38. *Navajo Mountain, Arizona,* c. 1947

39. *Navajo woman, Wide Ruin, Arizona*, c. 1948

40. *Hopi Buttes, Arizona,* c. 1942

41. *Monument Valley, Utah,* c. 1960

42. *Chorus, Indian ceremonial dance, San Ildefonso Pueblo, New Mexico,* c. 1929

43. *Sunrise, Old Walpi Pueblo, Arizona,* c. 1942

44. *Kiva and clouds, Taos Pueblo, New Mexico,* c. *1929*

45. *Winnowing grain, Taos Pueblo, New Mexico, c. 1929*

46. *Pueblo Indian man, New Mexico,* c. 1937

47. *Spanish-American woman, northern New Mexico*, c. 1937

48. *Spanish-American youth, Chama Valley, New Mexico,* c. *1937*

49. *Adobe dwellings, northern New Mexico, c. 1958*

50. *Santuario de Chimayó, New Mexico,* c. 1950

51. *Retablo, Santuario de Chimayó, New Mexico*, c. 1960

52. *Interior, Santuario de Chimayó, New Mexico,* c. 1960

53. *St. Francis Church, Ranchos de Taos, New Mexico,* c. 1950

54. *Chapel, Hernandez, New Mexico, c. 1939*

55. *Moonrise, Hernandez, New Mexico, 1941*

56. *Cross and thundercloud, near Truchas, New Mexico, c. 1960*

57. *Spanish-American man, northern New Mexico,* c. 1929

58. *Spanish-American woman, northern New Mexico,* c. 1929

59. *White cross and church, Coyote, New Mexico, c. 1960*

60. *Gravestone detail, Coyote, New Mexico,* c. *1960*

61. *Gravestone detail, Coyote, New Mexico,* c. *1960*

62. *Penitente Morada, Coyote, New Mexico,* c. 1950

63. *Interior, Penitente Morada, Espanola, New Mexico, c. 1930*

64. *Church, Cordova, New Mexico, c. 1950*

65. *Gate and cross, Canyoncito, New Mexico, 1961*

66. *Adobe ruin, Abiquiu, New Mexico*, c. 1941

67. *Church, Las Trampas, New Mexico,* c. 1950

68. *Churchyard, Tumacacori Mission, Arizona, 1952*

69. *Detail, facade, Tumacacori Mission, Arizona,* c. *1952*

70. *El Capitan Peak, Guadalupe National Park, Texas,* c. *1942*

71. *Detail, Papoose Room, Carlsbad Caverns National Park, New Mexico,* c. *1942*

72. *Burro Mesa and the Chisos Mountains, Big Bend National Park, Texas, 1942*

73. *Sand bar, Rio Grande, Big Bend National Park, Texas, c. 1942*

74. *Boquillas, Mexico, from Boquillas Canyon Overlook, Big Bend National Park, Texas,* c. 1942

75. *Near Gunlock, Utah, 1953*

76. *West Temple, Zion National Park, Utah, 1961*

77. *Near Mount Carmel, Utah, 1961*

78. *The Great White Throne, Zion National Park, Utah, 1942*

79. *Waterfall, Zion National Park, Utah,* c. 1947

80. *Farm, Autumn, southern Utah,* c. 1940

81. *Martha Porter, pioneer woman, Orderville, Utah*, c. 1961

82. *Mormon temple, Manti, Utah,* c. 1948

83. *Gravestone figure, 1891, L.D.S. Cemetery, Orderville, Utah,* c. *1961*

84. *Cedar Breaks National Monument, Utah*, c. 1947

85. *Mullein, southern Utah,* c. *1941*

86. *Salt Flats, near Wendover, Utah,* c. 1941

87. *Dune, White Sands National Monument, New Mexico,* c. *1942*

88. *Involute cactus, Saguaro National Monument, Arizona,* c. 1952

89. *Young cactus, Saguaro National Monument, Arizona, c. 1960*

90. *Organ Pipe Cactus National Monument, Arizona,* c. *1952*

91. *Papago girl, Mission San Xavier del Bac, Tucson, Arizona, c. 1950*

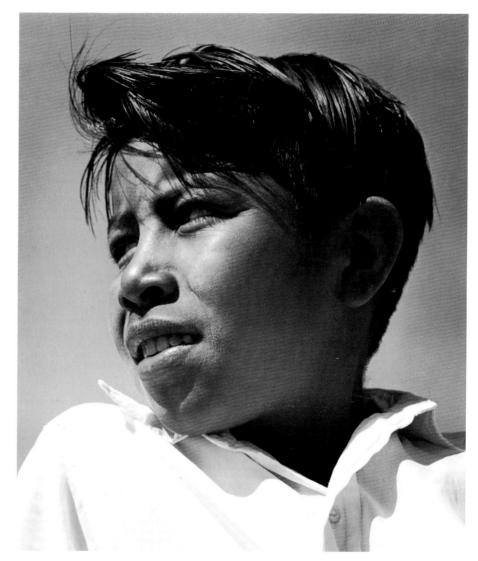

92. *Papago boy, Mission San Xavier del Bac, Tucson, Arizona, c. 1950*

93. *Thunderstorm, Mission San Xavier del Bac, Tucson, Arizona,* c. 1948

94. *Arches, North Court, Mission San Xavier del Bac, Tucson, Arizona, c. 1968 (Portfolio VII)*

95. *Veiled figure, Las Trampas Church, New Mexico, c. 1961*

96. *Aspens, northern New Mexico, 1958* (*Portfolio VII*)

97. *Inscription Rock, El Morro National Monument, New Mexico, c. 1950*

98. *Base of West Arch, Rainbow Bridge National Monument, Utah,* c. *1942*

99. *Pumice slope and pine trees, Sunset Crater National Monument, Arizona,* c. 1947

100. *Dead trees, Sunset Crater National Monument, Arizona,* c. *1947*

101. *Thunderstorm over the Great Plains, near Cimarron, New Mexico,* c. 1961

102. *Pioneer mill, Cimarron, New Mexico, c. 1961*

103. *Cottonwood tree, near Santa Fe, New Mexico,* c. 1961

104. *Windmill and thundercloud, New Mexico, c. 1958*

105. *Autumn storm, near Peñasco, New Mexico, c. 1958*

106. *Agathlán, near entrance to Monument Valley, Arizona,* c. 1960

107. *Tree and clouds, Tucson, Arizona,* c. 1944

108. *High clouds, Golden Canyon, Death Valley National Monument, California,* c. *1947*

LIST OF PLATES

109. *Flowers, Canyon de Chelly National Monument, Arizona, c. 1952*

Edited by Tim Hill

Designed by Paul Q. Forster, San Francisco

Type set by Lawton Kennedy, San Francisco
   Monotype composition by Mackenzie-Harris, San Francisco

Separations by George Waters, San Francisco

Printed by The Meriden Gravure Company

Paper supplied by S. D. Warren Paper Company

Bound by A. Horowitz and Son